WICCA
BOOK OF
SHADOWS

A Beginner's Guide to Keeping Your Own Book of Shadows and the History of Grimoires

BY LISA CHAMBERLAIN

Published by **Wicca Shorts**

ISBN: 1517610494

ISBN-13: 978-1517610494

Disclaimer

No part of this publication may be reproduced or transmitted in any form or by any means, mechanical or electronic, including photocopying or recording, or by any information storage and retrieval system, or transmitted by email without permission in writing from the publisher.

While all attempts have been made to verify the information provided in this publication, neither the author nor the publisher assumes any responsibility for errors, omissions, or contrary interpretations of the subject matter herein.

This book is for entertainment purposes only. The views expressed are those of the author alone, and should not be taken as expert instruction or commands. The reader is responsible for his or her own actions.

Adherence to all applicable laws and regulations, including international, federal, state, and local governing professional licensing, business practices, advertising, and all other aspects of doing business in the US, Canada, or any other jurisdiction is the sole responsibility of the purchaser or reader.

Neither the author nor the publisher assumes any responsibility or liability whatsoever on the behalf of the purchaser or reader of these materials.

Any perceived slight of any individual or organization is purely unintentional.

YOUR FREE GIFT

As a way of showing my appreciation for purchasing my book, I'm giving away an exclusive, free eBook to my readers—*Wicca: Little Book of Wiccan Spells*.

The book is ideal for any Wiccans who want to start practicing magic. It contains a collection of ten spells that I have deemed suitable for beginners.

You can download it by visiting:

www.wiccaliving.com/bonus

I hope you enjoy it.

CONTENTS

INTRODUCTION

As the religion of Wicca continues to grow, it draws new people from a wide variety of religious (or non-religious) backgrounds. While some are actually born to Wiccan parents, most are deliberately choosing the path for themselves.

Some have described themselves as atheists or agnostics before discovering Wicca. Many others were raised in one of the dominant religions of Judaism, Christianity, or even Islam. Their reasons for leaving their inherited religion can vary widely, but often people who come from more formal religions find that Wicca offers a more independent and spiritually authentic experience.

For one thing, Wicca doesn't tell you exactly what you must think, believe, or do.

It has its cardinal laws, like the Threefold Law and the importance of respecting other people's free will, but there are no detailed rules about how to live one's life, as there are in other faiths, and there is no single "divine source" commanding its followers.

For another, there isn't a specially designated "holy" day of the week that stands out from all the other days. This is refreshing particularly to those whose former spiritual lives involved going to church on Sundays and then essentially forgetting about religion for the rest of the week.

This is not to say that Christianity, or any other religion, isn't lived by its practitioners at every moment. But it's fairly easy, by comparison, to devote one day a week, plus holidays, to Christianity or Judaism and feel that there's not much more to it than that.

Wicca, on the other hand, is an every day religion, woven into the fabric of the lives of its practitioners.

It doesn't take place in a specially-designated building (with possible exceptions if a coven so chooses to own or rent one), and it doesn't revolve around a single, strictly-male deity who stays removed from the Earth plane. It also doesn't restrict participation in ritual to specific leaders, while everyone else sits together and observes.

Wiccans generally take a much more hands-on, active role in developing and practicing their spirituality. The use of rituals, spells, circle-casting, and working with nature all keep each of us attuned to the God, Goddess, and Earth in an intimate manner, where true magic actually lives and everything in our surroundings has its own breath.

One of the most important differences from the big monotheistic religions, of course, is that Wicca doesn't have one specific holy book, or "scripture," that its followers adhere to.

Instead, the tales, myths, spells, magical correspondences, and other ideas that relate to Wicca have been passed down through the generations and come from various sources—oral traditions, occult systems from various cultures, communications from spirits coming through to us via channelers, and other practitioners' writings. (You could probably make an argument that the holy texts of the "Big Three," — especially the Bible, are also made up of these things, though with less cross-cultural influence and also considered to be the end-all be-all of what believers are meant to pay attention to.)

Since there is no one single text for Wiccans to follow, practitioners are left to themselves to discover and collect information as they see fit.

This is where the Book of Shadows comes in.

Yes, there are key books that discuss Wiccan beliefs, traditions, and philosophy at great length and are definitely worth reading, but so many spells and styles of rituals practiced today were derived from the Book of Shadows of one Witch or another, so that a truly amazing variety of practices and information is available to learn from. The Book of Shadows is where the real "hands-on" quality of Wicca can really blossom, as practitioners navigate their own paths to learning and growing spiritually.

While those belonging to covens may have a more formal approach to spiritual texts that they adhere to as a group, it's highly beneficial for any and all practitioners to keep at least one Book of Shadows as a reference guide for their work, spells, rituals, correspondences, and new discoveries.

Of course, not all Wiccans feel this to be a necessary step in their journey, but it can truly be a useful—if not essential—resource. It is both a record of your own personal spiritual journey and an encyclopedia unlike any other.

This guide is all about creating and keeping your own Book of Shadows.

It will cover the history of this special book, its typical content, various options for creating and personalizing your own version, and even suggestions for modern-day incarnations of this venerable tradition.

Remember, however, that while this guide can be a very useful resource, you always have the freedom as a practitioner to decide for yourself whether something is relevant or right for you.

The advice and the options presented within these pages are simply guidelines, so if at any point you feel it best to do something differently, listen to your heart and follow what your higher self is telling you. There is no better compass.

Let this be a helpful resource for you and whoever you may choose to pass it on to, and may it help you along on your Wiccan journey.

Blessed Be.

HISTORY OF THE BOOK OF SHADOWS

THE ORIGINS OF THE BOOK OF SHADOWS

If you're new to Wicca, the phrase "book of shadows" probably sounds pretty mysterious.

Some people think the word "shadows" suggests some sort of negative content, since shadows can be thought of as things to fear or avoid.

But if you know anything about Wicca, you most likely know that it doesn't involve using magical power in any harmful way. And if you're reading this guide, you probably aren't afraid of shadows.

But what exactly is a Book of Shadows, and why does it have such a mysterious name? And what makes a Book of Shadows a Book of Shadows?

The answers to these questions can depend on who you ask, since Wiccans come from many different traditions, each with their own perspective on the subject.

But a quick look at the known history surrounding this type of book, including how it came to get its name, will help you get a basic sense of what we mean when we talk about a Book of Shadows.

THE GRIMOIRE: AN ANCIENT TRADITION

Written instructions about all things magical have been in existence for as long as humans have been able to write.

The earliest examples that have survived the ages—magical incantations found on stone tablets, talismans, and other objects in ancient Mesopotamia and Egypt—were created thousands of years ago.

References to magical texts can also be found in the Bible—although generally in the context of people burning them in order to leave their old ways behind and follow the Christian deity. But even as the early Christian Church grew in influence, many people continued to practice magic and write and read about occult subjects, even if they were less open about it than they would have been in the days before Christianity.

In fact, although we tend to think of the rise of Christianity as the "end of magic" in a broad sense, recent times, there was actually more of a coexistence between Paganism and the early Church than most people realize. In fact, it has been argued that the chief writers and readers of grimoires in the Middle Ages were members of the clergy!

Once the printing press was invented and started to become more accessible, magical texts began to be printed and distributed much more widely. At the same time, people still made them by hand, since handmade books of magic were considered to hold their own power as physical objects.

But before the printing press could make magic too accessible to the masses, the Roman Catholic Inquisition arrived to start punishing people for owning these books. The Witch Hunts that followed in many European countries led to the destruction of countless magical manuscripts, and any that survived were carefully guarded in secret. No one wanted to be caught with one, now that it could be punishable by death!

Despite the risks, though, books of magic continued to be produced right up through the late 19th century, which is when English occultists began forming different magical organizations, like the Hermetic Order of the Golden Dawn and Ordo Templi Orientis.

These groups collected as much occult information as they could, studied many ancient magical systems and developed ceremonial magical practices of their own. Their work had a significant influence on the development of what became modern Wicca, although the specific details of their practices were kept secret from non-members.

This secrecy, of course, became a Wiccan tradition in and of itself, and is still followed by many covens and solitaries, though not by all.

It was during the 19th century that the kinds of books written and studied by occultists began to be called "grimoires."

One early influential text that came to serve as a sort of model for the modern grimoire was The Magus by Frank Barrett, published in 1801. The Magus was a collection of magical theory and practical instruction drawn from ancient and medieval sources that Barrett hoped would reignite the practice of magic in his day.

He updated and modified some of the material from the older sources in order to make it more appealing and understandable to what was, at that time, a "modern" audience. This could be where the idea of "personalizing" the Book of Shadows got its start—we take what we know from the old traditions, and then make it our own in a way that works for us!

At any rate, by the 18th and 19th centuries, the "grimoire" came to be understood as a collection of information on occult subjects that might include any combination of the following: instructions for spellwork, including ingredients, ritual actions, and incantations; invocations to deities and other unseen entities; magical symbols; divination systems and techniques; and magical uses of herbs, crystals, shells, and other elements of the natural world.

These books were generally blends of different influences and time periods, along with original material based on the personal experience of their authors. Any given example of a classic grimoire may or may not contain everything mentioned above, and might contain other types of information not mentioned here, but these were the general characteristics of what came to be called the "grimoire."

Incidentally, the word grimoire is French in origin, but can actually be traced further back to the Latin grammar, which used to refer to learning of all kinds—not just languages. Subjects to be learned in those ancient days of Latin included occult knowledge, such as astrology and magic, so it makes sense to think of a resource for learning magic as a grimoire!

These days, if you look up "grimoire" in a dictionary, it is indeed usually defined as a book of magic spells and invocations. But some definitions mention invoking "demons," which definitely casts them in a different light.

It's key to realize that "demon" didn't always refer to an evil spirit. It was at one time a neutral word to describe any non-human entity that could be called upon to aid in magic. Since Christianity turned its back on magic, however, the word "demon" generally has very negative connotations.

Maybe someday these older definitions for "grimoire" will be properly updated. Either way, as a Wiccan, you have a nice alternative name for your own version of a magical book!

ENTER THE "BOOK OF SHADOWS"

In the late 1940s, when the religion now known as Wicca was beginning to take shape, one of its principal founders, Gerald Gardner, formed a coven called Bricket Wood. This was the first coven of what later came to be called "Gardnerian Wicca."

Gardner kept his own version of a grimoire for use in the coven, with rituals and spells that he would add to as he developed his own study and experience.

He didn't have a known title for this collection of material at the beginning. At least one early draft was called Ye Bok of Ye Art Magical, but it wasn't discovered until after his death. It seems he was still figuring out, at first, how he wanted to go about the creation and use of magical information that he compiled himself, as opposed to relying entirely the grimoires of others.

During this time, according to the coven's High Priestess Doreen Valiente, Gardner saw an article titled "The Book of Shadows" in an occult magazine, which was on the page opposite an ad for his own novel High Magic's Aid.

The article was about an ancient divination manual involving the length of a person's shadow, but Gardner was apparently inspired to use the term for a new type of grimoire—one that was written specifically for use in his coven, that would carry on the age-old tradition of keeping such spell books into the 20th century.

The "Book of Shadows" concept then expanded from Gardner's coven to other early offshoots of Wicca, such as Alexandrianism, and eventually became a widespread tradition of covens and solitary Wiccans alike.

Some Traditional Wiccans still use a Book of Shadows very similar to Gardner's, while others have adopted the spirit of the tradition, but created their own content.

SHADOWS AND SECRECY

There is a great deal of mystery surrounding the practice of Witchcraft in earlier centuries. This is largely due to the massive campaigns to eradicate any belief systems and practices that would compete with Christianity.

Driving Witchcraft underground, as we know, led to the loss of untold quantities of information on magic and other occult systems—not just because books were burned and Witches executed, but because practitioners now had to work in total secrecy in order to protect their lives and livelihoods.

Although these more severe threats eventually went away, it was still important during Gardner's time, and even for decades to follow, to keep the practice of Witchcraft a secret, unless practitioners wanted to be scorned, ostracized, or suspected of mental imbalance.

They had to keep their beliefs and works "in the shadows," including their catalogs of herbal magic, astrology, spells, and any other information still considered to be taboo in mainstream society. So it's not surprising that Gardner was attracted to the idea of a "Book of Shadows."

As for the tradition of keeping such books secret, however, much has changed since Gardner's day.

The covens that grew out of the original Bricket Wood, which generally used Gardner's original Book of Shadows, tried to keep the text unavailable to the uninitiated. But versions of it have been published many times in the decades since—as you will find easily with a quick internet search!

It is said by some that Witches are meant to have their Books burned upon their deaths, and this may in fact have been true of Witches in prior centuries, but in our more enlightened times this seems to be more of a symbolic act than a practical one.

In fact, some people share their Books of Shadows quite openly, even on the internet! So it's really up to individual Witches to decide whether to follow the tradition of secrecy (unless of course they belong to covens that have their own rules).

Depending on your circumstances, you may or may not need to (or wish to) keep the evidence of your practice a secret. But as to those in the past who chose not to burn their texts, and especially to those who passed them on openly, the Witches of today are grateful to have the knowledge!

MODERN DAY WITCHCRAFT AND THE BOOK OF SHADOWS

When it comes to covens, the Wiccan Book of Shadows tends to function like Gardner's did back in the mid-twentieth century.

These books traditionally contain rituals, spells, and information that is important to the coven. Some covens follow the "original" Book of Shadows as passed down from Gardner's tradition, but may also keep an additional book specific to their own practice. There may be a record of the significant events in the lives of members of the coven, such as handfastings and births or deaths.

Often, and especially in covens that stick closely to "hereditary" traditions (like Gardnerian Wicca), the coven's Book of Shadows is shrouded in a lot of secrecy. There may be only one copy of the book, kept by the coven's High Priestess. There is a belief that these original books hold the most powerful spells and rituals, and must be guarded carefully from anyone not initiated into the coven.

In other covens, each member will have their own copy of the coven's Book of Shadows. Others will even allow for their members to keep their own personal, unique Book of Shadows, so long as they include the rites and spells the coven uses, for the sake of consistency.

Their leaders may oversee the contents of it in some way, in order to prevent malevolent sorcery or other unwanted energies in the group's work. As you can see, there are all sorts of specifically prescribed practices that covens will follow, and because of the "group" orientation to Wicca that covens provide, they are by design more rigid in their approach than solitary practitioners are likely to be.

By contrast, solitary practitioners have the utmost freedom in terms of how they create their Book of Shadows.

There is no High Priestess or coven telling them what to include or omit, which colors to use or what material their book should be made of, or whether they are allowed to have one at all. They can make one book, several books, or separate books for each area of expertise. They can also include other entries like poetry and drawings in their book that may not be directly related to magic but still hold a great deal of personal power.

The sky is the limit, really. There is no "wrong" in Wicca, just "different." As long as they remember the cardinal rules of the Threefold Law and harming none, solitary Witches are entirely free to do as they please.

It's important to note here that there are also Wiccans—both solitaries and covens—who shy away from doing spellwork at all, and only use their Book of Shadows for rites and documenting the events of each Sabbat and Esbat. They may have recipes for key components of their rituals, such as holy water or incense, but the focus here is on the formal elements of the religion and not on magic.

THE WHYS AND WAYS WICCANS USE THEIR BOOK OF SHADOWS

The modern Witch may have one Book of Shadows or a collection of them.

There can be a master copy with tried-and-true information accompanied by a working document to record new "experiments," or a Witch may decide to put anything and everything into one massive book.

Regardless of the form it takes, modern-day Witches will use a Book of Shadows much like those who came before us.

Their pages consist of magical correspondences, recipes, spells, journal entries, poetry and music, rituals, sigils, and general notes.

They're an especially important part of a new initiate's time in the circle. This is because a newer practitioner will need something to refer back to for information that others already know by heart. Something like casting a circle may seem second nature to experienced Wiccans, but a beginner will need a guide for at least the first few forays into the circle.

Then there is ritual and spellwork.

Spells can be effective or ineffective, and they sometimes need tweaks or adjustments you would be unable to keep track of if you hadn't written the spell in your book for future reference.

In addition, some spells have elaborate wording and multiple steps, so it is much better to come into your circle with your trusty Book of Shadows in hand than to interrupt the energy by cutting out and then back in after looking up the answers to your questions.

One example of spellwork that almost always calls for a Book of Shadows is a form of enchantment, or "glamoury," which is much like a recipe you would use in cooking. The only difference is that you wouldn't be eating your creation, but using it to spritz on your hair or for washing your face.

These recipes are difficult to commit entirely to memory, and since this is fairly advanced magic, you want to be sure not to make any mistakes!

Almost every form of alternative spirituality and healing involves a journaling mechanism of some sort.

For example, there is so much to know about herbs and crystals: their magical, medicinal, and therapeutic properties.

Astrologers can appreciate this too because they would be lost without a lunar almanac, charts, correspondences, and ways to interpret the stars above us.

As you see, it would be pretty difficult to remember every single beneficial thing to know when practicing magic, and that's why every Witch can benefit from keeping a Book of Shadows.

CREATING YOUR BOOK OF SHADOWS

GETTING STARTED

Because a Wiccan Book of Shadows is so precious to its owner, the amount of effort you put into creating your own will lend power to your work and make it that much more invaluable and special to you.

You can definitely purchase Wiccan authors' compilations, and they usually contain everything under the sun you could ever possibly require information on, but they're also quite large and can be full of things you may or may not care about at all. It's very easy to get lost and go into information overload when reading these types of volumes.

Don't despair though. Being Wiccan doesn't mean you have to know every single magical correspondence by heart or be able to sputter off random facts or rites on command.

You will have your own paths of study you would like to follow, and those may differ greatly from 70% of what's found in a published grimoire. This is just fine! Remember that there is no single "end-all-be-all" source of information when it comes to Wicca.

Perhaps you do want to pursue learning absolutely everything as soon as possible, but via a method that's more effective for you with a method of organization you can configure for yourself. Sometimes published books are quite puffy and have a lot of fluff in between the meat and potatoes, so you may wish to condense what you see in them.

Whatever your plan may be, it will serve you well to make your own Book of Shadows that focuses only on the information that's relevant to you.

CHOOSING YOUR MATERIALS

Although it can be tempting to go the fancy route and get an ornate book with gold gilt pages, your first Book of Shadows should be attractive, yet mostly practical.

Think about its weight, size, and whether the pages are lined for orderly writing, or are smooth, clean, and blank.

Will you be able to carry the book with you when you go out into nature? Is it so flashy that it looks like it belongs in a museum? Will it draw unnecessary attention to you when you take it to the forest for some meditation?

If you're in a coven, what are their criteria for a member's book?

Convenience can be another concern for Witches. If you want to start learning right away, you may not feel it prudent to make your own book.

On the other hand, some will feel deep within themselves that the making of their book is a precious and spiritual experience that can't be replicated with a store-bought book.

Meditate on these questions within a circle, and look within to see what is right for you.

Once you've spent time considering these factors, you can make a more sound decision about what the best approach to the Book of Shadows looks like for you.

PRE-MADE JOURNALS AND STORE-BOUGHT BOOKS

Pre-made journals can be gorgeous. Some have dates, page numbers, gold-gilt or silvered edges for the pages, and elaborately tooled leather covers with some of the most beautiful and evocative designs you could imagine.

Other store-bought journals may have more modest designs, but sturdy covers—and possibly even snap closures—to protect the contents inside.

Truly, pre-made books really can be the bread and butter of all of the grimoires a Witch may create during a lifetime.

Indeed, there really is no limit to the kinds of journals and other "empty" books you can purchase online, at your local stationery, or even at a big-box store that will work just fine.

Some of these can also be taken to a book shop where you can have your name or a label of some sort embossed onto their covers, and book binders can take custom orders for special types of paper, too.

These can be an excellent option when you have no interest in spending an inordinate amount of time fashioning your Book, but would still like to personalize it to some extent.

There are dream journals, gardening journals, five-year diaries, blank books of all sizes and persuasions, coil-bound, key-tab—I could go on! There are so many options that it's often difficult to make any sort of decision at all!

Many Witches find that coil-bound books with hard covers are best for a basic Book of Shadows. They lay flat, have enough weight to stay put outdoors on an altar, and often come with lined paper for neater and more legible entries.

The bigger, classically-bound books are great for master copies when you want to make yourself a legacy chronicle or finally compile one big book of spells or rituals.

However, you may want to spring for the professional book binder when looking at these: again, they can blend blank pages with lined pages so you can include sigils, symbols, and records of alphabets, etc. much easier.

The only drawback with traditional bindings is that they are less practical in outdoor settings, and the pages tend to want to turn on their own while you're working your rituals and spells.

Let's not forget that you can keep smaller, more basic notebooks to record your work and correspondences until you have an idea of how you want to organize an official grimoire.

These are great because they often come with multiple tabs that separate subjects from each other, and they're coil-bound too—which, as already mentioned, is excellent for laying books flat or folding them over themselves for space-saving while you work at your altar.

Speaking of multi-tab notebooks, you might want to try the little chunky ones that are no more than four inches tall and can fit in a small handbag.

Sure, they're a little small for rituals or highly-involved spells, but they are great for making your own correspondence pocketbooks for herbs, the zodiac, divination, and more. Plus they are wonderful for creative writing, which is a common skill among Neopagans, and a great way to work toward writing your own spells!

DIY AND SEMI-DIY BOOKS

While convenience is important to many Wiccans when it comes to creating a Book of Shadows, you can also take the do-it-yourself approach and make your own. This can be a very spiritually rewarding process.

How much you do on your own can depend on your type of creativity—not all of us are skilled in bookmaking, after all—as well as what your intuition tells you is best for you.

Some people will go with a store-bought book and create their own cover over top of the original, and/or coat the edges of the pages in a non-transferable dye. There are others who have immense crafting skills and know how to tool leather and/or bind their own books.

Of course, there are plenty of in-between options.

For example, you may come across a type of journal that sits within a leather sleeve, with tooled leather Celtic knot-work on the front and gold metallic corner protectors. This type of book comes ready for page inserts that you can order according to your preference—either blank, lined, or a combination of both!

If you are truly ambitious and invested in making your own Book of Shadows, you can do so with nearly any material for a cover, any type of paper, and any style of binding.

The binding would come at a cost, of course, but it's well worth it if you've got a finished volume just begging to be bound.

Doing your own binding would mean a higher quality of paper, a knack for sewing or using glue, and at the very least, the ability to braid string, not to mention a plentiful quantity of patience.

Many people can do basic types of bindings, but unless you're quite practiced at it, they don't tend to last nearly as long as when you take it to a professional bookmaker.

WRITING IMPLEMENTS AND PAPER QUALITY

As you can probably imagine, people like Nostradamus or those who wrote the hieroglyphs in the Book of the Dead most likely used a quill and inkwell to produce their works. While there are many magic shops that sell quills and ink, these are used more for actual spellwork than for the writing of a Book of Shadows.

In the modern era, ink from inkwells doesn't dry fast enough (even the quick-dry varieties). It smudges, it stains clothes, and it can be generally unpleasant to work with if you're discovering the beauty of the quill for the first time.

Needless to say, using a quill is an art form and takes a ton of practice.

A great alternative to the inkwell that's a bit easier to use is the calligraphy pen.

You can get ink for these in a variety of colors and use a fancy fountain pen for them all. The ink in calligraphy pens tends to dry a tad faster, but for free-flowing ink, you have to have good quality paper that can absorb it without bleeding through.

If you have trouble with the point on a fountain pen, gel pens are the next best option.

Gel pens come in an immense array of colors and can be a cost effective option for both spellwork and general use. They usually don't bleed through paper, but they do run and leak from time to time, so it is best to stick to good quality gel pens that you would come across in an office supply store, rather than hitting up the locate bargain bin. Cheap gel pens tend to run dry quickly, and can have air bubbles in them that make them fail intermittently, which is annoying to say the least!

If your head's already spinning from all of these suggestions, grab yourself a package of ballpoint pens and work with those instead. You may want to opt for erase-able pens, but that isn't completely necessary.

Many people find that bolder pens are more comfortable to write with and leave a better look on each page than fine point pens that can fade more quickly due to depositing less ink with each stroke.

Pen grips can be helpful, as well. If you're more familiar with typing than writing by hand, you may want to try a few different types of pens on scratch paper until you find what works best for you.

DOING ARTWORK IN YOUR BOOK

It's traditional for a Book of Shadows to include the important sigils, symbols, and illustrations you encounter on your spiritual journey, as these prove useful in spellwork, visualizations, and good old general inspiration.

You may choose to render these simply, in rough-sketch form, or you might include color, details, and labeling. The choice is all yours, but you may want to consider this aspect while choosing supplies for your Book of Shadows.

Sketch pencils and sketch pads are an excellent pair of tools for drawing your symbols and other illustrations. White pearl erasers are also recommended—they work the best at erasing unwanted lines completely.

While you may very well feel confident sketching your pictures straight onto the pages of your book, you can also work on a separate piece of paper until you get an image you're satisfied with, and then paste it in. Fine liners (or fine-tipped Sharpies) are perfect for outlining finished sketches and adding bold lines to your drawings, and you can use gel pens or fine-tipped felts for colored symbols.

As for coloring in illustrations of animals, flowers, herbs, and other special objects, try using pencil crayons, watercolors, wax crayons, or felt markers. Pastels are gorgeous and rich in color, but they transfer to other pages easily and smudge like no one's business, so keep those for magic or creating artwork instead.

Again, some felts can bleed through paper, so this is another good reason to do your art in another book and paste it into the master copy once everything's dry and finished. You can also avoid felts bleeding through paper by using children's washable felt markers that deposit less color onto the paper. Plus, they won't stain your hands or clothing if you're doing some serious art!

If you decide to draw first in a separate sketch pad, you will also want scissors, a ruler, and glue.

The type of glue you use will dictate how long the piece of paper will adhere to your book's pages and whether it will be a detriment to the ink and paper because of the chemicals in it. Acid-free glue sticks are best because of this issue, but you can also get acid-free glue dots that work well for attaching just about anything into a book.

A handy rule of thumb to follow: if it's safe for scrapbooking, use it as much as you like in your Book of Shadows.

SECTION THREE

USING YOUR BOOK OF SHADOWS

STARTING OUT

Now that we've covered what kind of supplies you will need and possible approaches to creating your Book of Shadows, there are a few other considerations to address: how to compile the book, whether one book or more than one is best for you, why it's important to keep it safe and secure, and some 21st-century options for creating a Wiccan grimoire of your very own.

As always, remember that this will be *your* Book of Shadows, and it should be approached in the way that works best for you.

KEEPING A MASTER COPY AND ROUGH DRAFTS

As previously mentioned, keeping rough copies of information for later entry into a master copy of your Book of Shadows is a wise approach, particularly for your first book.

This is a very important step for a lot of beginners because they may want to change parts of spells or rituals once they've had some experience. Adding and/or removing specific elements of ritual, spell ingredients, etc. is much easier to do in rough drafts than in a final copy.

Also, this way you can sift through and add different bits of information—such as the magical properties of a certain herb or an ideal blessing chant for a particular Sabbat—as you discover them, and then catalog your entries properly later on.

If you plan on entering all kinds of information into your book and want to keep it well-organized while you work on rough drafts, you can use the multi-subject notebooks described above—that will help keep things in their place before you create the master copy.

A three-ring binder also works wonders because you can swap out the positioning of pages in order to keep things in logical order. Just be sure to get those little stickers that keep loose leaf paper from tearing out of the binder at random.

Either way, a master copy is the "nice copy" that you can put in an elegantly designed cover (or many such covers, depending on your approach). These can be then used when you've hit your stride as a Wiccan and have amassed many spells and a wealth of pertinent data.

Master copies are also important if you work in a coven that allows you to keep your own book combining the rituals and spells of the coven with your own information.

You will also find that there can be a lot of note-taking going on as beginners watch the High Priestess work with the other senior members of the coven during their first few times in the circle. These notes can be entered into your book too, if permitted by your group. (Remember, some covens forbid certain "information-sharing practices" because of privacy concerns.)

So as you can plainly see, having one book as a permanent home for your work after it's been perfected is very helpful. It can mean the difference between a neat and organized Book of Shadows or a scribble-ridden, tattered, rough-draft type of grimoire.

However, it's likely that you'll end up adopting your own version of continuing to use both types, since a Witch is never really done learning, no matter how practiced she or he becomes.

KEEPING MULTIPLE VOLUMES

In these modern times, with ever-shortening attention spans and constantly evolving ways of accessing and storing information, some practitioners of Wicca may struggle to make the best use of a single-volume Book of Shadows.

It can be cumbersome to be wading through information pertaining strictly to coven work when you are really just looking to do a simple solitary sabbat ritual, and it makes little sense to have to thumb past pages of divination tool correspondences in a book you wish to only spell-cast from at present.

Depending on your preferences, learning style, and personality, you may benefit from keeping multiple volumes, or separate books for separate purposes.

Many Wiccans like to keep several books and divide them into categories. One book will be for spells, another for magical uses of herbs, a third for rituals, a fourth for divination, journaling—and so on. You can even color code each book, so that herbalism is a green book, for example, and rituals a silvery blue.

This method has unlimited potential for keeping your resources well-structured and organized. It also allows you to work until you have enough information in each to make a large grimoire on a particular subject or group of subjects.

Of course, it's not necessary to keep multiple books, but it definitely helps when you've come to collect a huge amount of data across several subjects and want to be able to access it without pawing through pages upon pages of stuff that's irrelevant to that moment in time! And it's a great way to keep yourself organized and on the ball when it comes to working in the circle.

MAGIC ALPHABETS

Some practitioners like to write their grimoires in one of many magical alphabets.

These alphabets are usually rooted in some form of ancient writing made for the purpose of protecting text from prying eyes—particularly those who would probably send someone to the gallows if they knew what was written on the page!

While we are now thankfully free of such dangers, some Wiccans find that there is magical value to the energy put into writing in a different alphabet that requires more time, care, and focused attention.

There are several older alphabets which we still have access to that are considered to be quintessential "magic alphabets."

Below is a look at a few of the alphabets Wiccans have used in their books of shadows.

You are bound to find a few ideas here for masking your work from unwanted readers without the need to cast a protection spell on your book. You can also use one or more of these alphabets to amplify spellwork that uses writing as part of the spell.

Of course, you're not limited to using an existing alphabet—if you're a "DIY" kind of person, see the suggestions below for making up your own!

Theban

Often referred to as the Witch's Alphabet, no one knows where Theban originated, but the magical alphabet was first read and translated in the 1500s. It's mentioned often in philosopher and theologian Heinrich Agrippa's de Occulta Philosophia, where he deduced that it was loosely based on Latin.

Many Wiccans feel that this is one of the most aesthetically pleasing forms of ancient script out there.

Malachim

Malachim is another magical alphabet that was published by Heinrich Agrippa back in the 16th Century. It is derived from both Greek and Hebrew, and its name is similar to a type of angel in Judaism.

Celestial

Celestial is very close to Malachim in appearance and was actually created by Agrippa. Also known as "Angelic

Script," it is considered by some to be the alphabet of the heavens, which came through Agrippa as a divine inspiration.

Numeric Codes

Numbers have very powerful symbolism and can be assigned in any order or arrangement to represent text.

You can follow the typical system, beginning with A to represent 1, or start at a random number like 22 and go from there. Just be sure to keep a key if you create your own system, since you might forget where you started later on.

You can also use traditional numerological correspondences—either the Pythagorean or Chaldean system—for letters, if you wish to skip creating your own code. These two systems are fixed, so you can rely on being able to translate your work any time, either through the internet or other print resources on numerology.

Slavic, Chinese, Japanese, or Arabic

If you are fortunate enough to be bilingual, you may have the ability to directly translate other alphabet systems' characters into English phonetic sounds that can be used to make an alphabet.

Better yet, why not write your book in your other tongue? If you're living in a mainly English-speaking place, the chances of someone translating it are slim, and you won't have to work so hard to write things down and read them back.

Homemade Alphabets

You don't have to follow any pre-established system when writing in a magical alphabet. In fact, sometimes the greatest power comes from an alphabet you create on your own.

Think of it like speaking in tongues, which can be both therapeutic and make you closer to your creator. You can use symbols and sigils from alchemy, astrological symbols, shapes, combinations of dots, morse code, or anything else that comes to mind and makes sense to you.

Again, just be sure to write down the correspondences somewhere safe for your own reference, should you decide to stop using it and want to look back at the sections or spells you wrote in your secret language.

KEEPING YOUR BOOK OF SHADOWS SAFE AND SECURE

Your Book of Shadows is an incredibly important document. It is a religious book full of occult mysteries, your spiritual work, thoughts, feelings, and so much more.

As a Wiccan, your Book of Shadows will have had a great deal of energy put into it, and it will serve as a very useful tool in all that you do with your religion and spiritual path.

As mentioned in the beginning of this guide, Gerald Gardner, the original coiner of the term "Book of Shadows", believed that a Witch's book was to be burned upon death.

Now, whether or not you arrange to have this done upon your final hour is a very personal decision. Some people don't agree that this is necessary in modern times where being Wiccan is much more socially acceptable.

Some Wiccans prefer to keep their books to pass down through the generations, while others haven't given it much thought at all.

It's purely up to you how you want to handle the future of your Book of Shadows, but know that you cannot take it with you, so unless you destroy it yourself, it will be found by those you leave behind. Make sure it is full of positive material used for building yourself and others up, in the true spirit of "harm to none!"

Regardless of what happens when you pass on, in the meantime you need to keep this precious book safe and secure at all times.

It is not a child's plaything or your dog's chew toy. Your Book of Shadows should be stored with all of your other altar tools since it will usually be sitting on your altar during all of your work within the circle.

It's advisable to wrap it in a soft cloth and keep it out of light in order to preserve it and keep its surface from getting damaged, scratched, or dinged by anything else in your cupboard or chest of magic tools.

You will also want to keep it hidden in order to protect it from being glanced at by people who have no business reading it. This goes not only for children but others as well. This book is something sacred for you and those whom you grant permission to look within it. If you wanted people to peruse it for entertainment or as a novelty, it would be a coffee table book, rather than a Book of Shadows.

A SPELL TO PROTECT YOUR BOOK OF SHADOWS FROM PRYING EYES

Here you will find a spell of protection for your Book of Shadows that banishes negativity while keeping its contents safe from harm and unwanted "sneak peeks."

You can perform this spell with an existing grimoire, journal, diary, or Book of Shadows, but it will also be of great help when you are about to begin a new one.

This spell is also very convenient and easy enough to do right after cleansing and consecrating your Book of Shadows.

You will need:

- Your Book of Shadows
- A silver or gold pen

Instructions:

Once you have cast your circle, begin by placing your Book of Shadows in the center of your altar.

You will then take the pen and draw a sigil of your choosing on the inner side of the front or back cover (or both). This sigil can be a pentacle, an alchemical symbol, or something you have designed on your own, but it should represent protection, as well as divinity. (You can also pick two symbols, if you are doing both the inside of the front and back.)

You might use a gold pen for a god symbol or the symbol of the sun, and a silver one for the moon or a triple goddess sigil.

Keep in mind the loving, healing, and protective power of the divine as you draw your symbol(s) on the inside cover(s).

When you are finished, close the book, take up your athame, and draw a pentacle as you say:

> *"With Earth, Water, Fire, and Air*
> *keep my writings pure and fair.*
>
> *Water, Fire, Air, and Earth*
> *Grant access to those from marriage and birth.*
>
> *Fire, Air, Earth, and Water*
> *Prevent malevolent eyes from using this book for fodder.*
>
> *Air, Water, Earth, and Fire*
> *Let nothing negative or unwelcome enter*
>
> *and by Akasha, so mote it be.*
> *Let this book be a perfect aide to me."*

At the end of this, tap the top of the book with your finger, wand, or athame three times and say:

"Great Goddess and God.
Hear my decree!

Let my works adhere
to the laws of three."

Now, you can continue on with your other work or close the circle.

This spell will allow only those designated by you to look at your Book of Shadows while keeping others out, and as is evident, it's really easy to do.

Just make sure that your motives are pure and that you keep the mood light while doing the spell—remember: like attracts like; light attracts light.

WICCA GRIMOIRES IN THE 21ST CENTURY

Because we have so much technology at our fingertips in this, the 21st century, there are even more ways to compile a Book of Shadows than one could ever have imagined back in 1949.

Like all things in this century, we are able to do far more with much less, and Wiccans now have an unbelievable amount of data we can readily access online. But some sources of information may be more useful than others, and each individual Witch will have specific interests and preferences.

Perhaps you're more into electronic sources of information and don't care to work with physical paper and ink, but still want your own personal collection of Wiccan wisdom. Why not make your Book of Shadows on your computer or in an application?

THE ADVANTAGES AND DISADVANTAGES OF USING TECHNOLOGY

There are several ways to use technology in making your book, each with its own advantages and disadvantages.

Before you get started creating an electronic grimoire, try to weigh your options carefully. You wouldn't want to begin creating a Book of Shadows in one medium only to find that you prefer to use another instead. Being well-informed about all the possibilities will help you avoid wishing you'd chosen differently halfway through the process!

It would be unrealistic to say that using technology for building a Book of Shadows is absolutely easier and better than creating a traditional book.

Your experience will greatly depend on certain factors, such as how competent you are with using a computer, whether you have the resources to get the software you want, and whether you can stick with it in the long run.

You also still need to be able to either print off or otherwise view your spells and rituals while in the circle. Indeed, there is a lot of forethought that goes into stepping into the 21st Century!

In terms of advantages, typing and then editing are far faster than writing everything down by hand, which can sometimes lead to illegible work, scratched-out entries, and hard-to-read "chicken scratch," particularly if you happen to have bad handwriting.

It's also much easier to copy and paste illustrations or symbols, which those who aren't skilled in drawing tend to appreciate.

Perhaps best of all, however, is that if you are planning on publishing your Book of Shadows online, you can collaborate with others, if you so desire. This is an excellent benefit to using the internet because it grants you open and ready access to ideas and information you may not have encountered yet.

However, it's fair to say that digital versions of a Book of Shadows aren't always practical.

As mentioned earlier, there's the access within the circle to consider. Bringing a tablet into the circle with the day's various energies all over it may not be a good idea, depending on what else you use it for, and having to clear your electronics for every single ritual may not be appealing.

Furthermore, you could spill wax, oils, or holy water on your device. (And on a related note, if you don't back up your computer or tablet, you could also permanently lose your Book of Shadows, which would be a complete shame!)

Finally, there's the question of the relative effort it takes to make a Book of Shadows with a computer. How much energy and feeling is put into a handcrafted grimoire as opposed to a digital copy? If this makes a significant difference to you, you may want to opt for sticking with tradition rather than adopting technology into your practice in this way.

BOOK OF SHADOWS SOFTWARE, APPS, AND ONLINE FORUMS

There aren't many software programs out there that are meant for use as Books of Shadows. The few that are available are usually free, but tend to come with poor ratings. They're also quite rigid and follow their own structure, so you won't be able to fully customize everything as you would with a handmade book.

However, those who are completely unsure about how to get started will find online templates helpful, and these can usually be downloaded for free and printed off or followed onscreen in a word document.

Of course, another option is to use your PC's word processor for creating a Book of Shadows. You can do so on both PCs and Apple devices. And you don't have to have Microsoft Office—there are tons of free word processors—both online and downloadable—that allow you to type up your data and copy and paste images to accompany the text.

You also have the ability to insert, delete, and otherwise revise your text, a task that's much more time-consuming when you write a Book of Shadows by hand.

Furthermore, these files can be backed up on an external hard drive, which eliminates the above-mentioned danger of losing your hard work in the event of an electronic catastrophe.

If you have access to a printer, your options are further multiplied.

Most printers also function as scanners and photocopiers, so you can scan in sigils and other images you'd like to include in your Book of Shadows. Printing is also an alternative to bringing your device into the circle—you can selectively print the spells, incantations, etc. that you need for a specific ritual.

Perhaps most importantly, you can have both electronic and physical copies of your Book of Shadows. In fact, you can create a physical book with the printed pages, for a "neotraditional" DIY approach, or even send them to a book binder!

These can be very beautiful with elegant fonts, various font sizes, borders, page numbers, cover pages, and illustrations you've created or copied from online sources.

You also have the option of choosing high-quality paper for a "fancier" feel, and can even choose different color paper for different portions of the Book—perhaps one color for herbal information, another for ritual formats, etc. Indeed, printing gives you the ability to experiment with various approaches to creating a unique, personalized and professional-looking manuscript.

As for apps, we all know that there are new and interesting little downloads popping up on a near-daily basis. This isn't only true for the mainstream public—these days there are apps for Wiccans and Neopagans, too!

Android and Apple have some great apps available that either share a grimoire with you or give you the ability to create your own from scratch, with the aid of a template. The only issue with these is the above-mentioned potential awkwardness of using electronic devices during time in the circle. If you use your phone to store your Book of Shadows, be sure to turn the ringer and any other alert functions to silent during ritual!

For those who don't care to follow the tradition of being secretive about their practice of Wicca, there are a great many forums and social groups online with areas where people can release their Book of Shadows for public use.

However, it's important to keep in mind that sharing your wisdom and experience with others may have social implications for you outside of the online community.

Remember that you do not want to have conflict with employers, coworkers, and/or family members because of your religion. It may be okay to practice Wicca, but other people can be easily offended by most anything they decide to, particularly when there's still so much misinformation about Wicca out there in the world.

So unless you're blessed with a thoroughly enlightened social sphere, family, and work atmosphere, it's advisable to use a pen name if you want to release your Book of Shadows in a public forum.

CONCLUSION

A Book of Shadows is probably the key piece of reference material a Wiccan can possess.

It carries everything you could possibly need to cast spells, perform rituals, engage in divination, work for healing, use herbs and crystals properly, etc.

More than that, the Book of Shadows serves as a log of all of your activities, where you can record what worked or was helpful. It's also a place to express your artistic side through any creative writing and/or illustrations that you wish to include in its charmed pages.

You can make these special books out of any material that can hold writing, have them bound by a professional book binder, create multiple volumes, and even create them on your computer.

The most important thing to remember above all else is that your Book of Shadows is yours. It has an immense amount of your energy within it, and that makes it a very personal document—one that chronicals your spiritual journey from your initiation into the Craft, your continued learning, and the your core beliefs that shape you as a Wiccan and as a person.

With this in mind, you should not omit material out of shame or fear—especially if this material is important in your development. Your Book of Shadows is yours and yours alone (if you want to keep it that way), and as such it should be a place that's free from judgement—never feel that you must leave something out because it may be considered "odd" or "different".

Remember, inside your Book of Shadows are your thoughts, your spells, and your beliefs, and this is your journey. It's completely your decision who you want to share this information with, which ideas resonate with you, and which path you wish to follow.

As long as you stay true to yourself and respect others, you can't go wrong.

I will leave you with that thought, as now it's time for you to continue on your own path. I hope this guide has helped you to understand the importance of a Book of Shadows in a Wiccan's journey, as well as showing you the many different options available to you for making your own.

It has been an absolute pleasure writing this book, and I hope you have enjoyed reading it. I wish you all the best on your journey and I hope your Book of Shadows is quickly filled with lots of enlightening content that you hold dear!

Thank you one more time for reading.

Blessed Be.

SUGGESTIONS FOR FURTHER READING

While this guide provides an extensive overview of the many ways in which a Book of Shadows can be created and organized, the actual content is another topic altogether.

Ultimately, of course, the content you keep in your Book of Shadows is up to you, but since you can hardly be expected to come up with spells, correspondences, etc. out of thin air (at least, not at first), it's important to read as much as you can about the various aspects of Wicca that will eventually be represented in your own personal grimoire. The very brief list of references below can get you started along the path.

Among these books, you'll find actual examples of Books of Shadows, as well as spells, rituals, and the like, that you may decide to borrow or adapt for your own practice. Those beginners who aren't inspired by the idea of literally making their own books may want to investigate the final two items on this list, which are actually blank books for you to write in.

Eason's version has lined pages, and some very helpful basic information in the introductory pages. Scarabeo's version is an attractive hardcover journal with blank pages. You can find these books online and in Wiccan,

Pagan, or other "New Age" shops. Happy reading and writing!

Ann Moura, *Grimore for the Green Witch: A Complete Book of Shadows* (2003)

Silver Ravenwolf, *Solitary Witch: The Ultimate Book of Shadows for the New Generation* (2003)

Cassandra Eason, *The Book of Shadows: A Personal Journey for Your Craft* (2014)

Lo Scarebo, *Wiccan Journal* (2009)

DID YOU ENJOY *WICCA BOOK OF SHADOWS*?

Again let me thank you for purchasing and reading my guide. There are a number of great books on the topic, so I really appreciate you choosing my guide.

If you enjoyed the book, I'd like to ask for a small favor in return. If possible, I'd love for you to take a couple of minutes to leave a review for this book on Amazon.

Your feedback will help me to make improvements to this guide, as well as writing books on other topics that might be of interest to you. Hopefully this will allow me to create even better guides in future!

OTHER BOOKS BY LISA CHAMBERLAIN

Wicca for Beginners: A Guide to Wiccan Beliefs, Rituals, Magic, and Witchcraft

Wicca Herbal Magic: A Beginner's Guide to Practicing Wiccan Herbal Magic, with Simple Herb Spells

Wicca Book of Spells: A Book of Shadows for Wiccans, Witches, and Other Practitioners of Magic

Wicca Book of Herbal Spells: A Book of Shadows for Wiccans, Witches, and Other Practitioners of Herbal Magic

Wicca Candle Magic: A Beginner's Guide to Practicing Wiccan Candle Magic, with Simple Candle Spells

Wicca Crystal Magic: A Beginner's Guide to Practicing Wiccan Crystal Magic, with Simple Crystal Spells

Wicca Moon Magic: A Wiccan's Guide and Grimoire for Working Magic with Lunar Energies

Wicca Essential Oils Magic: A Beginner's Guide to Working with Magical Oils, with Simple Recipes and Spells

Wicca Elemental Magic: A Guide to the Elements, Witchcraft, and Magical Spells

Tarot for Beginners: A Guide to Psychic Tarot Reading, Real Tarot Card Meanings, and Simple Tarot Spreads

Wicca Magical Deities: A Guide to the Wiccan God and Goddess, and Choosing a Deity to Work Magic With

Wicca Wheel of the Year Magic: A Beginner's Guide to the Sabbats, with History, Symbolism, Celebration Ideas, and Dedicated Sabbat Spells

Wicca Living a Magical Life: A Guide to Initiation and Navigating Your Journey in the Craft

Magic and the Law of Attraction: A Witch's Guide to the Magic of Intention, Raising Your Frequency, and Building Your Reality

Wicca Altar and Tools: A Beginner's Guide to Wiccan Altars, Tools for Spellwork, and Casting the Circle

Wicca Finding Your Path: A Beginner's Guide to Wiccan Traditions, Solitary Practitioners, Eclectic Witches, Covens, and Circles

Wicca Book of Shadows: A Beginner's Guide to Keeping Your Own Book of Shadows and the History of Grimoires

Modern Witchcraft and Magic for Beginners: A Guide to Traditional and Contemporary Paths, with Magical Techniques for the Beginner Witch

FREE GIFT REMINDER

I'd hate for you to miss out, so here is one final reminder of the free, downloadable eBook that I'm giving away to my readers.

Wicca: Little Book of Wiccan Spells is ideal for any Wiccans who want to start practicing magic. It contains a collection of ten spells that I have deemed suitable for beginners.

You can download it by visiting:

www.wiccaliving.com/bonus

I hope you enjoy it.